KINGFISHER
READERS

level
3

Volcanoes

Claire Llewellyn

 **KINGFISHER**

First published 2012 by Kingfisher
an imprint of Macmillan Children's Books
a division of Macmillan Publishers Limited
20 New Wharf Road, London N1 9RR
Basingstoke and Oxford
Associated companies throughout the world
www.panmacmillan.com

Series editor: Heather Morris
Literacy consultant: Hilary Horton

ISBN: 978-0-7534-3058-3
Copyright © Macmillan Publishers Ltd 2012

9 8 7 6 5 4 3 2 1

1TR/1011/WKT/UNTD/105MA

A CIP catalogue record for this book is available from
the British Library.

Printed in China

Picture credits
The Publisher would like to thank the following for permission to reproduce their material. Every care has
been taken to trace copyright holders. However, if there have been unintentional omissions or failure to trace
copyright holders, we apologize and will, if informed, endeavour to make corrections in any future edition.
Top = t; Bottom = b; Centre = c; Left = l; Right = r
Cover Science Photo Library (SPL)/Jeremy Bishop; Pages 5 Shutterstock/Vulkanette; 6 Corbis/Vince Streano;
7 Corbis/Gary Braasch; 10 Getty/Colin Anderson; 12–13 Corbis/C. Brad Lewis; 13 Corbis/Michelle Garrett;
15 & 16 Amy Nichole Harris; 17 Alamy/The Art Gallery; 18 Corbis/Paul Souders; 19c Shutterstock/David P.
Lewis; 19b Shutterstock/Andy Z; 21 Getty/Mike Theiss; 22 SPL/Anakaopress/Look at Sciences;
23 SPL/Jeremy Bishop; 24–25 Shutterstock/zschnepf; 25 Shutterstock/nikolpetr;
26–27 Corbis/Bo Zaunders; 27 Corbis/Bob Grist; 28 NASA/JPL.

Contents

What is a volcano?

A volcano is a mountain. Most of the time, it looks like any other mountain, but now and again it throws out **gas**, **ash** and burning rock. This is called an **eruption**.

The biggest eruptions are like firework displays. There is a lot of noise and red-hot rock shoots out of the **peak**.

Why do volcanoes **erupt**? Where does the hot rock come from? This book tells you about the wonderful world of volcanoes.

Did you know?
The word volcano comes from the name Vulcan. Vulcan was the Roman god of fire.

A volcano erupts

Mount St Helens is a volcano in the
United States of America. In the spring
of 1980 it looked like any other mountain.
Snow and ice covered its peak and thick
forests grew all over its slopes. The forests
were home to deer, wild cats and other
animals. The mountain looked like a
very peaceful place.

On the morning of 18 May, Mount St Helens suddenly erupted. There was a huge **blast** and great clouds of smoke shot out of its peak. The snow and ice quickly melted, and rivers of water ran down the hillside.

Volcanoes in numbers
Before the eruption, Mount St Helens was 3,000 metres high.

After the eruption

This is a picture of Mount St Helens one week after it erupted. The mountain looks very different. Part of its peak was blown away and a hole was blasted in its side. The snow and ice have all gone.

The forests were knocked down. Many animals were killed and 57 people died.

An erupting volcano is one of the most powerful things on Earth.

Can you see how Mount St Helens changed? Look back at the photo on page 6.

Volcanoes in numbers
Mount St Helens is now only 2,500 metres high.

Inside a volcano

Inside every volcano there is a tall hole shaped like a chimney. It goes deep down inside the Earth. It is so hot there that some of the rock has melted.

This hot, runny rock is called **magma**. Sometimes it rises up the hole in the volcano, pushes out of the ground, and makes a big hole called a **crater**. The hot rock that comes out is called **lava**.

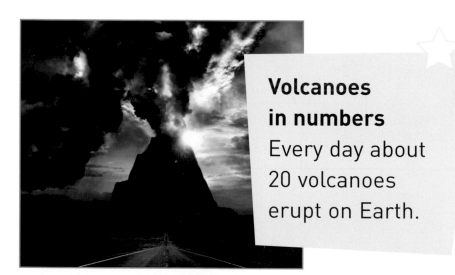

Volcanoes in numbers
Every day about 20 volcanoes erupt on Earth.

The lava pours downhill, cools and hardens. Every time the volcano erupts, a new layer of lava pours out. The layers build up into a **cone**.

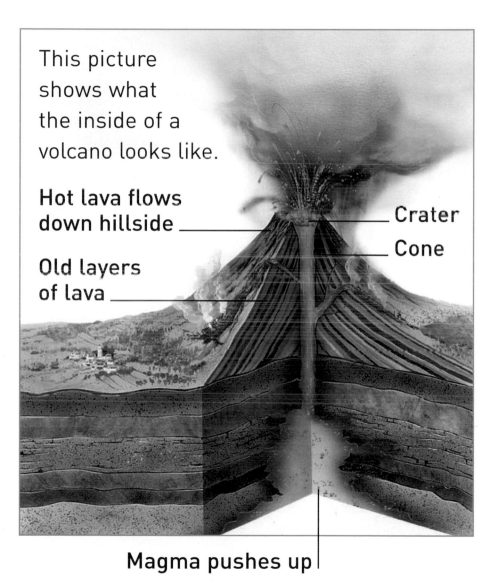

This picture shows what the inside of a volcano looks like.

Hot lava flows down hillside

Old layers of lava

Crater

Cone

Magma pushes up

Run for your life!

Volcanic eruptions are not all the same. In some eruptions, lava **seeps** out slowly and gas comes out in puffs. Other eruptions are like a bomb going off!

People nearby have to run from the rocks that shoot out and could crush them. They run from the ash that coats everything with

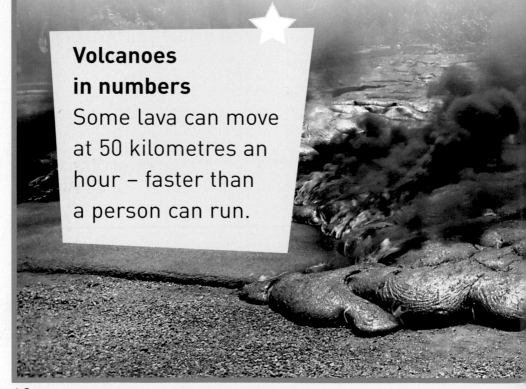

Volcanoes in numbers
Some lava can move at 50 kilometres an hour – faster than a person can run.

dust and from the gases that make it hard to breathe. They run from the burning lava that destroys farms, villages and roads.

This house in Sicily has been buried in lava.

A story from the past

About 2,000 years ago, a volcano in Italy suddenly erupted. It was called Mount Vesuvius. The volcano was near a town called Pompeii (say 'Pom-PAY').

One afternoon the townspeople heard a loud bang. They looked up and saw

a cloud of ash shoot
out of the top of
Mount Vesuvius.
Soon after, the town
was hit by falling rocks.
People ran out of their houses, but they
could not breathe in the clouds of gas
and ash. By evening, thousands had died.

The next day, more ash and lumps of
lava poured over the town. They hardened
into rock, and Pompeii was hidden.

Today Mount Vesuvius overlooks the ruins of Pompeii.

The hidden town

Pompeii lay hidden for 1,500 years.
Then one day, people who were digging
a well came across some old ruins.
They were the ruins of Pompeii.

Soon teams of people came to dig. They
found old streets, shops and fine houses.

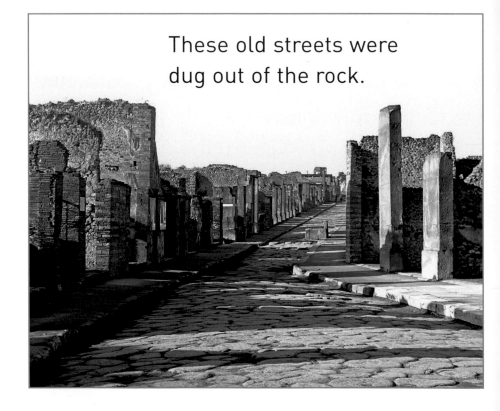

These old streets were
dug out of the rock.

This wall painting shows a Roman baker with loaves of bread.

They found **bronze** statues and wonderful paintings. The digging went on. More than half the town has now been dug out of the rock. Today people from all over the world visit Pompeii to see what life was like in the past.

Volcanoes in numbers
More than two million people visit Pompeii every year.

Three sorts of volcano

There are hundreds of volcanoes on Earth. They can be sorted into three groups.

1. Active volcanoes

Volcanoes that erupt quite often are active volcanoes.

This volcano on Iceland erupted in 2010.

Volcanoes in numbers
Earth has more than 1,500 active volcanoes.

2. Dormant volcanoes

Some volcanoes have not erupted for a very long time. They are dormant volcanoes. They seem to be asleep, but they could wake up!

Mount Callaghan is a dormant volcano in Canada.

3. Extinct volcanoes

Some volcanoes are very old and will never erupt again. They are extinct volcanoes.

Diamond Head is an extinct volcano in Hawaii.

Volcanoes under the sea

Volcanoes under the sea erupt in the same way as volcanoes on land. Lava pours out of a hole in the sea bed. It cools in the water and hardens into rock. The layers of lava build a cone, and this grows a bit higher every time the volcano erupts. The tallest cones stick out above the water and make an island in the sea.

The highest mountain on Earth is an undersea volcano. It is called Mauna Kea and it is 10,200 metres high – that's 1,350 metres higher than Mount Everest!

The bottom of Mauna Kea is under the sea.

Studying volcanoes

Some people study volcanoes and try to **predict** when they will erupt. These **experts** measure the size of a volcano to see if magma under the ground is making the mountain swell. They check to see if the ground is getting hotter.

Volcano experts work in dangerous places. They have to wear special heat-proof clothes. They crawl into craters to collect rock, ash and gas. Their work is important and saves lives.

Visit a volcano

Most volcanoes are safe to visit. If you walk to the top, you can look down into the crater. You may even smell the gases from inside the Earth. They smell like rotten cabbages and eggs!

Crater Lake is an extinct volcano in the United States. It last erupted 8,000 years ago. The deep lake is full of clear water which is perfect for sailing or swimming.

Walkers explore a volcano in Japan.

Did you know?
Crater Lake is 597 metres deep. It is the deepest lake in the United States.

Crater Lake is now a national park for everyone to enjoy.

Volcanoes are useful

Some people live on active volcanoes.
They do this because the ash that
volcanoes throw out makes the soil
good for farming.

The water
in this lake
in Iceland is
heated by
volcanic rocks.

Volcanoes are useful in another way. The rocks in the ground around them are very hot. People use this heat to warm their homes, schools and swimming pools. Heat from volcanoes is free and it never

runs out. In Iceland it is even used to grow bananas.

Growing bananas in Iceland.

Volcanoes in space

You will find volcanoes all over our planet. If you could travel into space, you would find them on other planets, too.

Jupiter has a moon called Io. The dots all over its surface are very big, active volcanoes. A volcano is erupting next to the orange area in the photo below.

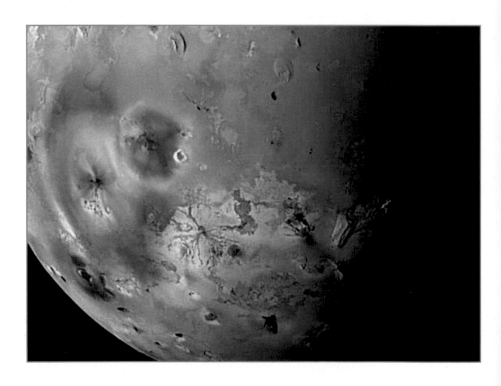

Olympus Mons is a volcano on Mars. It is 27km high – about three times higher than Mount Everest!

Active volcanoes remind us that just below the hard, rocky surface there is melted rock. Even Earth, our own planet, is not as solid as it seems!

Glossary

ash The soft, grey dust that is left after a fire.

blast A big bang or explosion.

bronze A red-brown metal.

cone The rocky, steep-sided shape of a volcano.

crater The bowl-like hole at the top of a volcano.

erupt To throw out lava, ash and gas.

eruption When a volcano erupts.

experts People who know a lot about something.

gas A very light, shapeless substance that is not solid or runny. Air is made of gases.

lava The hot, melted rock that comes out of a volcano.

magma The hot, melted rock inside the Earth.

peak The pointed top of a mountain.

predict To say what will happen in the future.

seeps Flows slowly.

Index